ALONG
PUZZLE TRAIL

150 Assorted Bible Puzzles and Facts for Children

based on quizzes in
THE BIBLE BULLETIN
a bi-monthly magazine for children
1993-2000

Along the Puzzle Trail
© Copyright 2001 Ian Brown

ISBN 1 84030 112 0

Ambassador Publications
a division of
Ambassador Productions Ltd.
Providence House
Ardenlee Street,
Belfast,
BT6 8QJ
Northern Ireland
www.ambassador-productions.com

Emerald House
427 Wade Hampton Blvd.
Greenville
SC 29609, USA
www.emeraldhouse.com

Introduction

The summer of 1993 saw the launch of The Bible Bulletin - a little bi-monthly magazine filled with puzzles, articles and competitions for children.

Over the past few years, requests have been received for all the puzzle material in the Bible Bulletin to be gathered together in one book. Therefore this publication.

Seven years worth of Bible Bulletin material has been compiled ... adding up to more than 100 Puzzles arranged under 5 main topics, with a further 30 articles of an educational and evangelistic nature also included.

The material has been arranged chronologically, beginning with a section on God's Creation, and progressing through Noah's Ark and The Flood, Old Testament History, New Testament History, and concluding with a General section.

While this book is designed to give hours of enjoyment and Bible teaching to children, it should also prove an extremely useful aid to Sunday School Teachers and Children's Workers.

My personal desire is that it may instill in many children an interest and love for God's Word, increase that interest in others and glorify the Lord whom we are all called upon to worship and serve.

Ian Brown   Londonderry, October 2001

Acknowledgments

None of us can ever be successful as a 'one-man-band.' In acknowledgment of that fact, I want to record my thanks to all who have shown an interest in the Bible Bulletin since its launch eight years ago. That must include the ministers who have promoted it within their congregations and, of course, the many children who have sent in their competition entries month after month - and written some impressive letters of thanks (I still have those - and treasure them). Thank you all most sincerely!

Special thanks is due to a number of individuals. First, to my printer for six years, William Healy. Until declining health forced him to withdraw from all printing work, Mr Healy had been of tremendous assistance in the work of the Bible Bulletin. I also appreciate the enthusiasm that John Dumigan showed for the project, always ensuring that the printed copies reached me in time for distribution. Thanks is likewise due to Gillian Ross, whose present involvement with the printing of the Bulletin has been a labour of love, and to Esther Mackey and Naomi Ritchie, who have spent considerable time wading through each of the puzzles contained in this book, checking that everything is in its proper place and offering valued suggestions.

No small measure of thanks is also due to my wife, Gillian, and family, for all their patience and encouragment - and to our gracious Lord, without whose help none of life's projects would ever be completed.

Contents

GOD'S CREATION

*Taking a look at
the Genius
and Greatness of the Lord*

... *some fascinating facts*

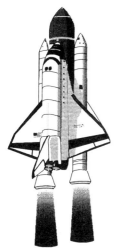

1 Your feet may be resting firmly on the ground, but water covers nearly three quarters of the world's surface.
PSALM 104:25: *"So is this great and wide sea, wherein are things creeping innumerable, both small and great beasts."*

2 The albatross bird has the widest wingspan. Its wings often measure more than 3 metres (10 feet) from tip to tail. How tall are you? Compare your height with the albatross.
PSALM 104:12: *"By them shall the fowls of the heaven have their habitation ... ."*

3 About 6000 stars are visible from earth without the aid of a telescope. See how many you can count in the sky tonight!
PSALM 104:19: *"He appointed the moon for seasons: the sun knoweth his going down."*

4 About 2000 thunderstorms are raging throughout the world at this moment. Lightning has flashed 500 times since you started reading this.
PSALM 104:3: *"... Who maketh the clouds his chariot: who walketh upon the wings of the wind."*

5 Our home in the universe, the Earth, is one of nine planets that orbit the sun; it is the only planet that can support life. When astronauts first saw the earth from space, they were amazed by the beauty of our blue planet.
PSALM 104:31: *"The glory of the LORD shall endure for ever: the LORD shall rejoice in his works."*

6 Forests cover 39 million square km (15 million square miles) of the planet's surface. Plants and trees take in carbon dioxide from the air and give off oxygen; without them there could be no life on earth.
PSALM 104:16: *"The trees of the LORD are full of sap; the cedars of Lebanon, which he hath planted."*

1 Where did Noah's Ark come to rest? (Genesis 8)

2 Where did Elijah make his great sacrifice? (1 Kings 18)

3 Where did Moses receive the Law from God? (Exodus 19)

4 Where did Abraham prepare Isaac for sacrifice? (Genesis 22)

[Letters in centre column are the same]

OUR GOD HAS MADE ...

Can you fill in the missing words in the puzzle below using the Bible verses listed at the side?

Isaiah 45:7

Amos 5:8

Psalm 95:5

Job 9:9

Psalm 104:26

G R E A T

MOUNT OF OLIVES

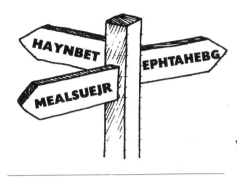

When He was on the Mount of Olives, Jesus sent two of His disciples to a nearby village to get a donkey. This signpost shows three other places that were close by - but someone has jumbled up the names. Can you unscramble them?

A QUESTION OF DISTANCE

How far was the Mount of Olives from Jerusalem?
(Acts 1 will help you.)

MOUNTAIN EXPERIENCES

Name three of Christ's disciples who shared some really special moments with their Lord on mountains?

CLUE: They were with Him on the Mount of Transfiguration and also in the Garden of Gethsemane (at the bottom of the Mount of Olives)

11

Unjumble the following words and you will discover the names of some famous Bible rivers

RONNA (Numbers 21)
NBAAA (2 Kings 5)
HE TARES UP (Gen. 2)
RONDAJ (2 Kings 5)
SKHION (Judges 4)
KJBOAB (Genesis 32)

_____   _____   _____

_____   _____   _____

RIVERS IN EDEN

How many rivers flowed out of the Garden of Eden?

3 ☐   4 ☐   5 ☐   6 ☐

KEY QUESTION NO.1

What was the name of the river where John was baptised?

(Check Matthew 3 for your answer)

    (a) PHARPAR
    (b) JORDAN
    (c) NILE

ANSWER:

[   ]

4 ... PLANTS

WHICH SHADOW MATCHES THE FLOWER?

CAN YOU FIND EIGHT BIBLE PLANTS/TREES IN THE WORDSEARCH?

```
S E E D S
Y L I L B
C E D A R
A X T U O
M Q N F S
O L I V E
R G M P N
E N R O C
```

ANSWER:

_____
_____
_____
_____
_____
_____
_____
_____

KEY QUESTION NO.2

What kind of FLOWER did Jesus mention when He was speaking about the glory of King Solomon? (Check ... Matthew 6 or Luke 12)

(a) ROSES
(b) POPPIES
(c) LILIES

ANSWER:

5 ... TREES

DOWN
1. Isaiah 44:14

ACROSS
1. Psalm 104:16
2. Ezekiel 27:15
3. Genesis 30:37
4. 1 Kings 19:4
5. Hosea 4:13
6. Psalm 45:8
7. Luke 19:4

TREES IN THE DESERT

In Isaiah 41:19, how many different kinds of tree does God promise to plant in the wilderness and the desert?

6 ... BIRDS OF THE BIBLE

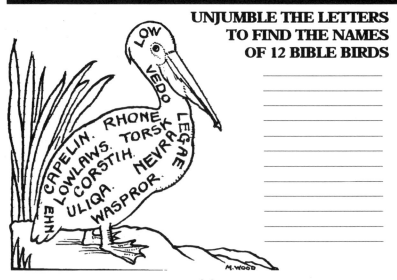

UNJUMBLE THE LETTERS TO FIND THE NAMES OF 12 BIBLE BIRDS

M. WOOD

7 ... DINOSAURS

*Many imagine that most of the dinosaurs were ferocious meat eaters. Fact is, about 95% of all dinosaurs lived on plants ... and, when they were created, they were ALL vegetarian!**

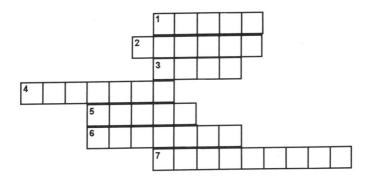

*(check Genesis 1:29&30).

CLUES DOWN:
1. Isaiah 44:14

CLUES ACROSS:
1. 2 Samuel 5:11
2. Isaiah 41:19
3. Isaiah 41:19
4. 1 Kings 19:5
5. Genesis 30:37
6. Genesis 30:37
7. Psalm 78:47

MEET LEVIATHAN!

LEVIATHAN is the name given to a real 'sea monster' which is described in the Bible. The 41st chapter of the Book of Job paints a picture of a creature that:
• lives in the sea (vs1&31),
• is covered by a spear-proof scaly armour (vs15-17,23,26-30),
• is incredibly fierce (vs8-10,25&33)
• and tremendously powerful (v12).

Perhaps the most amazing thing about leviathan is that it was able to breathe fire! Job 41:19-21 tell us: *"Out of his mouth go burning lamps, and sparks of fire leap out. Out of his nostrils goeth smoke, as out of a seething pot or caldron. His breath kindleth coals, and a flame goeth out of his mouth."*

Many of the fire-breathing dragon legends may come from creatures like this one. It could have been a Kronosaurus (a great dinosaur-like sea reptile) or a similar type creature that God created on Day 5 along with all the other fish and marine life.

KEY QUESTION NO.3

What is the name of the creature which Job describes in the 40th chapter of his book? Is it:

(a) BEHEMOTH
(b) LEVIATHAN
(c) TYRANNOSAURUS

ANSWER:

[   ]

WHO WAS HERE FIRST?

WHICH OF THE FOLLOWING CREATURES
HAVE BEEN ON EARTH THE LONGEST?

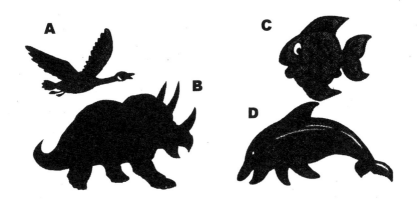

SPOT THE DIFFERENCE!

*Look carefully at the two drawings of dinosaurs above.
The pictures have 10 differences - some obvious,
some not so obvious. Can you find them all?*

DINO JOKES

Q: Why didn't the Tyrannosaurus skeleton attack the museum visitors?
A: *Because it had no guts!*

Q: What do you call a blind dinosaur?
A: *I-don't-think-he-saurus!*

Q: What do you get when you cross a dinosaur with fireworks?
A: *Dinomite!*

Q: What do you get if you cross a dinosaur with a CD-Rom?
A: *A mega-bite!*

Q: What do dinosaurs put on their chips?
A: *Tomatosaurus.*

Q: What happened when the dinosaur took the train home?
A: *His mummy made him take it back!*

Q: What do you call a dinosaur that steps on everything in its way?
A: *Tyrannosaurus Wrecks.*

Q: What did the dinosaurs put on their floors?
A: *Rep-tiles.*

Q: Which type of dinosaur could jump higher than a house?
A: *Any kind! A house can't jump!*

Q: What do you call a group of people who dig for fossils?
A: *A skeleton crew.*

Q: Which dinosaur slept all day?
A: *The dino-snore!*

8 ... THE HUMAN BODY

UNJUMBLE THE WORDS BELOW,
ALL OF WHICH FORM PARTS OF YOUR BODY

1. chatmos
2. clumses
3. snobe
4. treasier
5. tojins

6. reath
7. seykind
8. dobol
9. slobew
10. sinestinte

SPOILING GOD'S DESIGN!

ALL THE WORKING PARTS of your body are organised by a control centre - the brain. God designed our bodies well, but sadly, people often do things which harm them. They sometimes become ill and even die, because they poison their bodies with things like tobacco, alcohol and other drugs. God is not pleased when people harm their bodies, for they are spoiling His design.

KEY QUESTION NO.4

Over 4000 years ago, Moses wrote: "The life of the flesh is in the blood." Where do we read these words?

(a) PSALM 90:10
(b) LEVITICUS 17:11
(c) GENESIS 6:17

ANSWER:

THE HUMAN SKELETON

INSIDE YOUR BODY is a framework of bones, called a skeleton. Without this you would be like jelly, and unable to stand!

A fixed skeleton would be of little use as you need to be able to move around. So your skeleton has a number of joints which allow you to move your legs, bend your knees and elbows, move your head, and bend down to pick things up with your hands.

These joints are moved by muscles which work when they receive messages from your brain.

Many machines, like a mechanical digger, have joints which have to be supplied with oil. Your joints are lubricated by a special liquid and protected by a cushion of gristle. Your system of bones and muscles is much more wonderful than any machine ever designed by man!

KEY QUESTION NO.5

King David made a fascinating comment about how the human body is made in one of his Psalms. Which one?

(a) PSALM 133
(b) PSALM 136
(c) PSALM 139

ANSWER:

OUR FIVE SENSES

The human body is a marvellous creation. The five senses of the body allow us to do some amazing things.

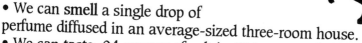

• We can **see** a candle's flame 30 miles away on a dark, clear night.
• We can **smell** a single drop of perfume diffused in an average-sized three-room house.
• We can **taste** .04 ounces of salt in 530 quarts of water.
• Our sense of **touch** can detect a pressure that depresses the skin .00004 inches on the face or fingertips.
• And we can tell where a **sound** is coming even when it arrives at one ear .0003 seconds before its arrival at the other ear.

AUTOMATIC FUNCTIONS

A normal man at middle age performs, among many others, the following automatic functions in each 24 hours ...
• his heart beats 103,680 times;
• his blood circulates every 23 seconds, and travels 168 million miles;
• he breathes 23,000 times and inhales 438 cubic feet of air;
• he digests 3-1/4 pounds of food, and assimilates over a half-gallon of liquid.
• he evaporates 2 pounds of water by perspiration;
• he generates 98.6 degrees heat, and generates 450 tons of energy;
• he uses 750 muscles;
• his hair grows 1/100 of an inch and his nails 1/200 inch;
• and he will use 7 million brain cells. And all these occur spontaneously and automatically!

Everyone has to agree the human body is *ingeniously designed!*

NOAH'S ARK & THE GREAT FLOOD

Salvation and Judgment

JESUS, THE SINNER'S ARK

We can think of the Lord Jesus Christ as an ark. God said to Noah: "Come thou and all thy house into the ark" (Genesis 7:1). Noah obeyed. He and his family were saved by entering into that ark while the rest of the world was drowned.

Christ Jesus says to you: "Come unto Me." (Check Matthew 11:28 & John 6:37). He wants you to be safe from the flood of God's anger that is going to fall on sinners. Will you come to Him today?

Come into this Ark, the sky grows dark,
There's a storm called 'God's Great Judgment Day':
From its fierce angry waves, in the Ark you'll be saved,
Come into the Ark today!

NOAH'S ARK WORDSEARCH

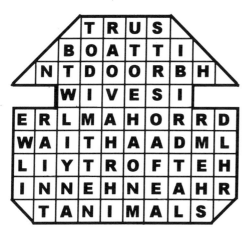

The letters left over spell out part of
PROVERBS 3:5.

Cross the following 10 words out of the WordSearch:
- *animal,*
- *bird,*
- *boat,*
- *door,*
- *forty,*
- *Ham,*
- *Noah,*
- *rain,*
- *Shem,*
- *wives.*

FACTS & FIGURES

... ABOUT NOAH'S ARK (Genesis 6:14-16)

1.			**P**				
2.			**I**				
3.			**T**				
4.			**C**				
5.			**H**				

1. Type of wood the ark was made from
2. Where the door was placed
3. Number of stories in the ark
4. Unit of measurement for the ark
5. The ark was 30 cubits in _____.

THE FLOOD WAS WORLDWIDE!

Some say that the Genesis Flood was quite small.
In Genesis chapters 6-10, words and phrases appear
more than 30 times which clearly show that the Flood
was WORLD-WIDE!

HOMING INSTINCT

Which path will lead the dove back to the Ark?

ANSWER:

KEY QUESTION NO.6

How many times did Noah send a dove from the ark?

(a) 1
(b) 2
(c) 3?

ANSWER:

ARK CROSSWORD

ACROSS

1. It happened in Noah's day
5. Noah's ship
6. A sheep does this
8. T__E (not false)
10. The rain lasted __ days (Gen. 7:4)

DOWN

2. At last Noah came to dry __ND.
3. Globe, sphere
4. Alright (slang)
7. The route of the raven - to and __.
9. Abraham was born here (Gen. 15:7)

DID YOU KNOW?

The ark was *so large* (1,400,000 cubic feet in capacity) that 520 railroad box cars could be fitted inside.

Only 150 box cars would be needed to comfortably carry 2 of each air-breathing creature in the world today! That's just 1 storey of the ark!

TWO BY TWO - FIND THE PAIR

Which two 'pictures' of Noah's Ark are the same?

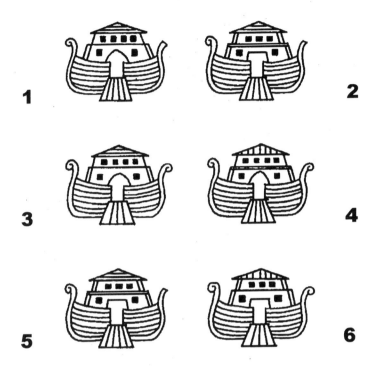

1   **2**

3   **4**

5   **6**

KEY QUESTION NO.7

During the Flood, God sent rain upon the earth
for HOW MANY days and nights?

- (a)   7   ☐
- (b)   40   ☐
- (c)   150   ☐
- (d)   224   ☐

Check your answer in Genesis 7:4&12

NOAH'S ZOO

Time to see who's a budding artist!

Noah led the animals into the ark two by two: can you turn the letters in 'Noah's Zoo' into some of the other animals?

DID YOU KNOW?

OUT OF THE ARK ... INTO A TENT!

The Bible tells us that Noah was the first man to live in a tent - after he had lived in the ark during the Flood.

The mouths of babes ROY MITCHELL

mum wasn't too pleased with her mother's day present, then?

no — and i must admit, i'm baffled — it was a big sacrifice for me...

... spiders like that don't grow on trees

OLD TESTAMENT HISTORY

*Meet Some of
the Men and Women
Who Counted*

1 ... JOSEPH

How much do you know about Joseph?
Try the clues below to fill in the crossword

All answers are in Genesis 41-44

CLUES

ACROSS

4 Another word for a feast
6 Joseph's younger brother
8 There was a _____ in Canaan
9 The brothers wanted to buy
___
10 The brother who offered to stay while the others got Jacob

DOWN

1 The country Joseph lived in
2 Joseph's father
3 This was found in Benjamin's sack
5 He was put in prison while the others got Benjamin
7 The governor of Egypt

What was the name of the Captain of Pharaoh's guard?

_____

A WONDERFUL COAT

Jacob made a coat of many colours (pieces) for his son Joseph.

Isaiah 61:10 tells us about some wonderful clothes that God our Father gives the one who trusts Him - *"the garments of salvation"* and *"the robe of righteousness."*

These are the best clothes of all!

MYSTERY:
WHY WAS JOSEPH IN PRISON?

Many things happen that we cannot understand.
I am sure Joseph wondered "why?" on the way to Egypt.
But God had an answer for all that happened
... it was covered in His plan!
cf. GENESIS 50:20; ROMANS 8:28

KEY QUESTION NO.8

How many pieces of silver did the Ishmeelite traders pay for Joseph?

(a) 10
(b) 20
(c) 30

ANSWER:

2 ... MOSES

Help Moses and the Israelites plot their path
to the Promised Land

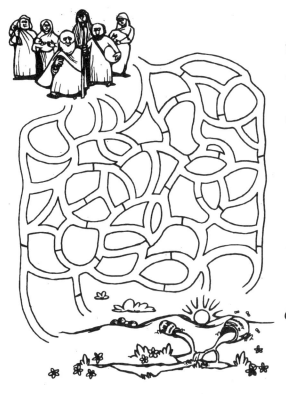

Heaven is the promised land for the Christian. We have wonderful word-pictures of it in John 14:1-3 and Revelation 21&22.

Are *you* going? Check John 3:3.

I'm bound for the promised land, I'm bound for the promised land: Oh, who will come and go with me? I'm bound for the promised land!

MOSES AND THE PSALMS

Moses wrote the first five books of the Bible - Genesis, Exodus, Leviticus, Numbers and Deuteronomy (called The Law or the Pentateuch).

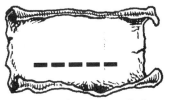

Moses' name also appears at the top of <u>ONE</u> of the Psalms ... which one?

35

MATCH THE SCROLLS

There are THREE PAIRS of scrolls in the drawing below.
Can you find all three pairs?

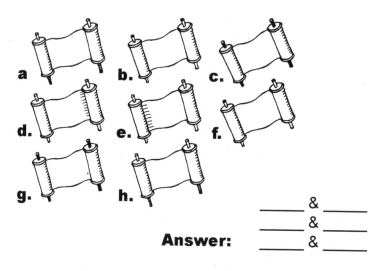

a. b. c.

d. e. f.

g. h.

Answer: _____ & _____
           _____ & _____
           _____ & _____

WHO WROTE THE FIRST FIVE BOOKS OF THE BIBLE?

**Genesis
Exodus
Leviticus
Numbers
Deuteronomy**

Some evil men refuse to accept that Moses wrote the first five books in the Bible.

However, our Lord Jesus Christ certainly believed that he did (look up Mark 7:10, Mark 12:26 & Luke 24:27).

We should too.

THE WORD 'PENTATEUCH'

Take the word

PENTATEUCH

How many words of 2 letters and more
can you make out of it?

☐ **Up to 35**   - Good
☐ **36-65**   - Very Good
☐ **66-98**   - Excellent
☐ **99+**   - GENIUS!

I got _____ words from "Pentateuch."

KEY QUESTION NO.9

How many chapters are in
the Pentateuch?

(a) 178
(b) 183
(c) 187

ANSWER:

There are 10 differences between the two pictures below.
Can you spot them all?

KEY QUESTION NO.10

*What was the total number of times
the people of Israel marched round
the walls of Jericho? (Joshua 6:3&4)*
(Put a Ring round the correct answer)

5   7   8   11   13   21

WORDS IN THE WALL

Can you fill in the missing words in one of Jericho's walls using the clues below (Answers in Book of Joshua)?

CLUES DOWN

1. Colour of thread Rahab used
2. Grandfather of Achan (7:1)
3. He stole a Babylonish garment
5. Short for advertisement
8. Number of days Israel marched round Jericho
10. Number of times Israel marched round Jericho on the second day (6:14)
11. Achan was Carmi's ___?

CLUES ACROSS

2. Great-grandfather of Achan (7:1)

[CLUES ACROSS CONTINUED]
4. Woman who hid 2 spies
6. Precious metal
7. Little city where Israel lost a battle (7:4)
8. A king of the Amorites (2:10)
9. Rahab asked the spies for a true _____. (2:12)
11. Number of days Israel went round Jericho once (6:3)
12. Signal to start
13. The spies left Rahab's house as this was being shut (2:5)
14. Father of Joshua (1:1)

39

A MESSAGE IN CODE

God gave a special message to Joshua when He called
him to serve Him. Using the code below, try to find out
what some of that message was.

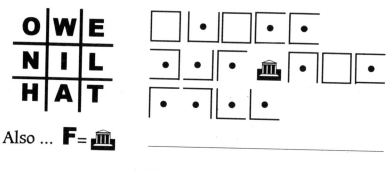

Also ... **F= 🏛**

_____

_____

JESUS IS THE WALL OF
PROTECTION TO HIS PEOPLE

While the walls of the wicked will always come down,
God has promised to be a wall to His people
(Zechariah 2:5).
How great His love and care must be to give
us this kind of protection!

Charles Fry (1837-82) rejoiced concerning Jesus:

*"He'll never, never leave me, nor yet forsake me here,
While I live by faith and do His blessed will;
A wall of fire about me, I've nothing now to fear,
With His manna He my hungry soul shall fill ... ."*

He was right. Is Jesus Christ your protector?

Samson was a really strong man. It is important to remember that he got his strength from the Lord. It was when *"the Spirit of the Lord came upon him"* that he did mighty things (Judges 14:6, 14:19, 15:14).

We do not look to Samson for our strength today, but to the Saviour. Philippians 4:13 assures us: *"I can do all things through Christ which strengtheneth me."*

WHICH TOWN IS IT?

Take the *first* letter of each of the objects in these pictures, and find the name of a town Samson visited.

1. _____
2. _____
3. _____
4. _____
5. _____
6. _____
7. _____
8. _____

☐☐☐☐☐☐☐☐

SOME STATS ABOUT SAMSON

1. How many sheets did Samson promise to those who could explain his riddle? (Judges 14:12)
2. The Philistines could not solve Samson's riddle before how many days? (Judges 14:14)
3. How many years did Samson judge Israel in the days of the Philistines? (Judges 15:20, 16:31)
4. How many Philistines did Samson kill with the jawbone of an ass? (Judges 15:15)
5. Samson told Delilah to bind him with how many green withs? (Judges 16:7)
6. Judges 13:1 tells us that the Lord delivered Israel into the hand of the Philistines - for how many years?

Total

The total sum of Questions 1-6 is the same number as the answer to 'Key Question No.11'

KEY QUESTION NO.11

WANTED

REWARD

How many pieces of silver did each Philistine 'lord' offer as a reward for the capture of Samson?

(a)   10
(b)   100
(c)   110
(d)   1100

Circle the correct answer (Check Judges chapter 16)

```
W O R K R U T H A R U
W T F O U X B B O A Z
O R I D T N A O M I B
R U E Y H A R A I S E
B I L R A M L H N R V
D Z D R P O E A A E I
O R I A R A Y R E K T
O E I M O A B V L R A
F E A N S A D E G O L
A N A T K R U S T W E
Z M E H E L H T E B R
```

Can you find the following words in the grid:

Ruth, Glean, Died, Naomi, Orpah, Field, Boaz, Eat, Workers, Moab, Drink, Work, Barley, Relative, Food, Harvest, Marry, Bethlehem, Sad

IMPORTANT MESSAGE FROM BOAZ

When Boaz told Ruth to stay in his field and glean, he gave her some instructions about eating. Problem is ... he's missed out all the vowels here: can you put them in?

_t m__ lt_m_
c_m_ th__
h_th_r, _nd
__t _f th_
br__d,
_nd d_p
thy m_rs_l
_n th_ v_n_g_r.

SPOT THE DIFFERENCE

Boaz arranges to marry Ruth
Can you spot 10 differences between the pictures?

WHICH HARVEST WAS IT?

Ruth and Naomi arrived in Bethlehem at the beginning of which harvest? (Check Ruth 1)

ANSWER:

Just about everyone knows the famous story of shepherd boy David versus the giant Goliath. On the next few pages, you have a lot of puzzles to solve about this story.

• Read 1 Samuel 16&17 for some help •

1 *The name of the shepherd*
2 *The name of the king*
3 *When the king felt ill, David played ____ for him.*
4 *David fought the giant _____ .*
5 *The king offered David a loan of his _____ .*
6 *But David _____ God and did not use it.*
7 *David wrote a song which says God is like a _____ who looks after us.*

BONUS PUZZLE

Rearrange the letters in the shaded boxes (above) to spell out the name of a Bible Book

MISSING PICTURE!

There was no such thing as photography in Bible times. Perhaps you could complete this 'newspaper' report by drawing the necessary picture?

Price
0.4 shekels   **THE BETHLEHEM TIMES**   No. 3471

Local Boy Defeats Giant

Recent reports from the frontline in the valley of Elah tell of an amazing Israelite victory. David, the local shepherd boy, has killed Goliath, the infamous giant soldier of the Philistine army.

Goliath, at nearly three metres tall, was almost twice the size of our young shepherd boy. Also, against the experienced Goliath's full armour, David came with nothing but his shepherd's sling as his weapon. Eyewitnesses claim that David was seen walking along a stream where he chose five smooth stones, exchanged a few battle cries with Goliath, and then, in one quick move, ran forward and hit the giant right between the eyes with an early volley from his sling. ❏

TRACE THE BIBLE VERSE

Can you find the words on the 'stones' and put them in the right order to get a great statement David made in the Valley of Elah? (Check your answer in 1 Samuel 17).

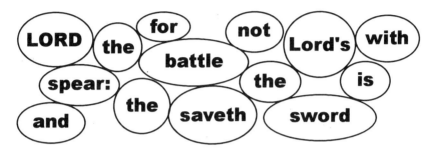

_____

_____

_____

KEY QUESTION NO.12

What did David bring to his elder brothers in the army? **(Answer in 1 Samuel 17)**

    (a) Lentiles, loaves and honey
    (b) Loaves, corn and cheese
    (c) Bread, milk and onions

ANSWER:

```
┌─────────────────────────────────┐
│                                 │
└─────────────────────────────────┘
```

WHICH ROUTE FOR DAVID?

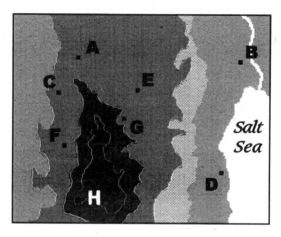

David is 'on the run' from king Saul. Starting from **A** (Gibeon), he wants to visit each location, eventually returning back to **A**. He plans to take a lengthy rest at **F** (Adullam) - and has arranged for supplies to be in place at **B** (Gilgal) so that he and his men can pick them up on the way through to Adullam. The problem is that David doesn't want to pass through any place more than once on his tour. Which route should he take?

MAP READING

Have another look at the map above. You have *not* been told the names of towns C,D,E,G or H. But you can find them by unscrambling the 'words' on the right! The first one (**C**) is done for you.

[A Bible Map will help]

(**C**) - HEAR JIJ MARKIT
= KIRJATH-JEARIM

(**D**) - DEEING
(**E**) - SAMUEL JER
(**G**) - THE BEL HEM
(**H**) - ROBHEN

JESUS THE ROCK OF REFUGE

The place marked **F** on the map opposite is Adullam. We are told in 1 Samuel 22:1&2 that David found refuge in a cave called Adullam. The Lord Jesus Christ is the refuge for all His people. He is a place of salvation - shelter - security.

The Lord's our Rock, in Him we hide,
A shelter in the time of storm;
Secure, whatever ill betide:
A shelter in the time of storm.
Oh, Jesus is a Rock in a weary land,
A shelter in the time of storm!

The question must be: have you received Him as your Saviour? Is He your Refuge?

DID YOU KNOW?

Scientists believe they have found the cave of Adullam: it meets all the requirements as given in the Bible.

KEY QUESTION NO.13

David wrote TWO of his psalms
when he was "in the cave." Which two?
(Tick the box beside the correct answer)

❑ Psalm 27 and Psalm 59
❑ Psalm 141 and Psalm 17
❑ Psalm 57 and Psalm 96
❑ Psalm 142 and Psalm 57
❑ Psalm 119 and Psalm 20

REARRANGE THE LETTERS

'Juggle' all the letters
in the 'strange' sentence
below to find a famous
line written by
the Psalmist David.

HE HELD STORMY RED SHIP

THE WORD "BLESSED"

*How many Psalms begin with
the word "Blessed"?*   5☐ 6☐ 7☐

KEY QUESTION NO.14

*Who was David's
great-grandfather?*

(a) Boaz
(b) Obed
(c) Jesse

ANSWER:

Esther is being crowned queen: how many differences can you spot between the two pictures? ☐

HOW MANY PROVINCES?

Esther 3:13 tells us that "letters were sent by posts into all the king's provinces, to destroy, to kill, and to cause to perish, all Jews, both young and old, little children and women."
How many provinces were there in the kingdom of Ahasuerus?

10 ☐   **27** ☐   **127** ☐

IN PRISON!

• What were the names of the two chamberlains of king Ahasuerus who plotted to kill him?

_____

• Were these men only put into prison for their crime?

_____

• Which man uncovered the plot to kill the king - and saved the king's life?

_____

[ALL ANSWERS IN ESTHER CHAPTER 2]

KEY QUESTION NO.15

Name the wicked man in the kingdom of Ahasuerus who hated the Jews and drew up an evil plan to have them massacred?

(a) Haman
(b) Hatach
(c) Bigthan

ANSWER:

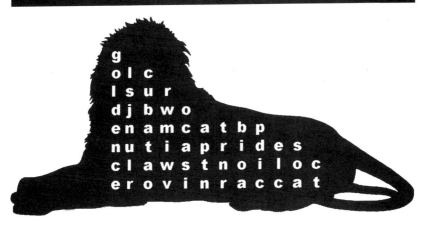

```
g
o l c
l s u r
d j b w o
e n a m c a t b p
n u t i a p r i d e s
c l a w s t n o i l o c
e r o v i n r a c c a t
```

Can you find the 9 words hidden inside the lion?
Tick the boxes below as you find each word.

cat	☐	cub	☐	claws	☐
carnivore	☐	golden	☐	lion	☐
mane	☐	prides	☐	roar	☐

KEY QUESTION NO.16

Who closed the lions' mouths so that they did not harm Daniel?

☐ The princes

☐ King Darius

☐ The Angel of the Lord

(You'll find the answer in Daniel 6)

How Many Days?!

Put a circle round the number of days it would have taken a traveller to walk from one end of Nineveh to the other. *(Jonah 3:3)*

40   11   7
1   3

A BOOK OF "GREAT" THINGS

Jonah is a book of "Great" things.
Can you find the great things that are in the following verses?

Jonah 1:4   _ _ _ ☐
Jonah 1:12   _ ☐ _ _ _ _ _
Jonah 1:17   _ _ ☐ _
Jonah 3:2   _ ☐ _ _
Jonah 4:2   _ _ _ _ _ ☐ _

Use the 5 letters that are boxed in above to discover where Jonah was sleeping in the ship:

☐ ☐ ☐ ☐ ☐

JUST A TALL TALE? ... NEVER!

Some say that the story of Jonah chapter 1 cannot be true because a whale could not swallow a man ... and, even if it could, the man would not survive.

However, several cases have been known when a whale has swallowed a man (sperm whales can swallow objects 4 feet in diameter) - and the man *has* survived!

One of the most famous involved the whaling ship 'Star of the East' in 1891. When near the Falkland Islands, a whale was sighted. Two boats were lowered. The men in the first boat managed to harpoon it. The second boat was overturned by the whale ... one sailor was drowned; another disappeared.
The whale was killed - and cut up. The next day, something moved in the stomach. On cutting it open, Bartle, the missing seaman, was found - unconscious, but alive.

Interesting though that story (and others like it) may be, we do not need it to believe what the Bible says in Jonah chapter 1. We do not believe Jonah chapter 1 because some men have survived for some length of time in the stomach - we believe it because God has told us so, and Jesus taught it to be true (read Matthew 12:39-41; Matthew 16:4).

OLD TESTAMENT "J" BOOKS

How many books in the OLD TESTAMENT begin with the letter J ?

4 ☐   5 ☐   6 ☐

A VITAL MESSAGE IN CODE

Using the grid on the right, find some tremendous words which Jonah spoke when he was in the belly of the great fish.

🌵 = D, 🌴 = L, 🏠 = O, ⛰ = V.

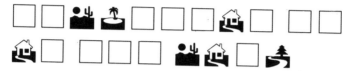

These words are found in JONAH __ verse __

JONAH WORDSEARCH

s	o	a	b	o	o	t	h	s	a	b
y	r	g	n	a	t	s	w	o	r	e
a	s	h	i	p	i	o	m	a	k	l
d	e	e	p	h	l	a	p	n	u	l
r	h	a	s	l	r	p	p	i	t	y
o	s	r	i	i	o	d	a	n	h	r
l	a	b	n	j	d	n	i	e	r	c
t	n	e	p	e	r	i	n	v	e	s
e	r	y	y	t	u	w	e	e	e	a
s	o	f	t	j	o	n	a	h	l	c
e	t	o	i	a	g	h	s	i	f	k
m	e	r	c	i	f	u	l	d	i	c
r	m	t	o	l	o	o	e	v	i	l
o	l	y	a	o	s	v	e	i	t	o
w	a	a	t	t	e	m	p	e	s	t
a	c	m	t	s	a	e	s	p	e	h

worm, gourd
Tarshish
tempest
ship, mariners
asleep, east
wind
Nineveh
belly, fish
billows, forty
sackcloth
repent, angry
Joppa, Jonah
merciful, deep
booths, pity
city, ashes
lost, flee
lots, three
Lord, evil
calm, die
cry, days

NEW TESTAMENT HISTORY

Getting to Know
some of the
People and Main Events

h	t	p	y	g	e	e	m
a	p	r	s	p	y	l	a
b	i	e	l	r	t	b	n
j	o	s	e	p	h	a	g
e	h	e	g	m	d	t	e
s	a	n	n	y	a	s	r
u	s	t	a	r	t	r	o
s	j	s	e	s	u	s	y

Can you find the following words in this special wordsearch about the Birth of Jesus?

• • •

Mary, Joseph, Jesus, angels, stable, manger, presents, star, Egypt

• • •

What *other* words appear in the wordsearch?

BIRTH OF CHRIST IN GOSPELS

How many of the gospels record the birth of Jesus? Is it:

(a) 2 (b) 3 (c) 4?

KEY QUESTION NO.17

Jesus grew up into manhood in which city?

(a) BETHLEHEM
(b) NAZARETH
(c) JERUSALEM

ANSWER:

DECODE THE SECRET MESSAGE!

How good are you at breaking secret codes?
Using the 'Pig pen code' below, work your way through
the secret message at the bottom of the page.
(The lines are the 'pens' and the dots are the 'pigs';
each letter has its own shape of pigs and pens).

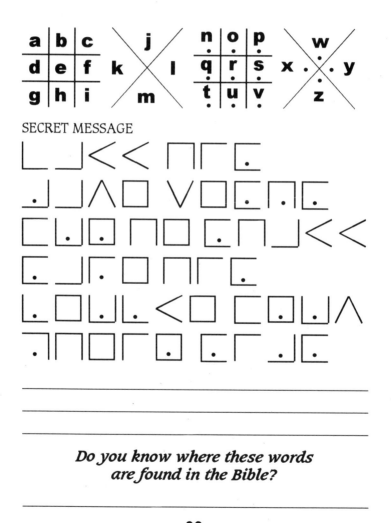

SECRET MESSAGE

Do you know where these words
are found in the Bible?

All 6 answers can be found in Mark 6:6-13

1. Another name for the followers of Jesus
2. The disciples wore these while travelling
3. Jesus taught them
4. The number of the disciples
5. Jesus had authority over this kind of spirit
6. Where the people lived

ARE YOU A DISCIPLE?

When I was at Sunday School, we used to sing a little chorus:

There were twelve disciples,
Jesus called to help Him ...
... We are His disciples,
I am one, are you?

The Lord Jesus is *still* looking for disciples: people who will learn from Him, love Him, obey Him and follow Him no matter where He leads them. I am one of His disciples. Are you?

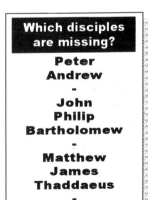

Which disciples are missing?

Peter
Andrew
-
John
Philip
Bartholomew
-
Matthew
James
Thaddaeus
-
Judas Iscariot

WHICH DISCIPLE?

Using the clues below, give the name of one of Jesus' disciples

◆ He wrote 2 of these .

◆ He owned a .

◆ A 🐓 crowed when he lied.

The disciples' name was [＿＿＿＿＿＿]

AS MANY WORDS AS YOU CAN!

Take the name

THADDAEUS

How many words of 2 letters and more can you make out of it?

☐ Up to 15   - Good   **I got**
☐ 16-25   - Very Good   ＿＿＿＿
☐ 26-39   - Excellent   **words**
☐ 40+   - GENIUS!   **from "Thaddaeus."**

Some words from the story of the feeding of the five thousand are hidden in the grid below.
Try to find them all.

p	r	a	y	c	s	h	i	p	m
d	a	n	t	h	s	u	s	e	j
s	e	i	t	i	c	t	e	s	h
m	s	s	f	l	o	a	v	e	s
e	e	t	e	d	t	k	w	l	g
m	v	i	w	r	s	a	c	p	r
b	a	s	k	e	t	s	g	i	a
r	o	k	v	n	l	e	i	c	s
l	l	a	u	k	l	v	v	s	s
w	o	m	e	n	u	a	e	i	e
l	j	h	s	i	f	o	o	d	f
h	s	e	v	a	o	l	h	n	b

Jesus
ship
sick
cities
desert
loaves (5)
twelve
baskets
five
fish (2)
disciples
grass
sit
pray
eat
full
men
women
children
give
food

Did you find all 5 "loaves" in this puzzle?

KEY QUESTION NO.18

How many fish did the little lad give to Jesus when the five thousand were fed? (Check Matthew 14).

(a) TWO
(b) FIVE
(c) SEVEN

ANSWER:

```
┌─────────────────────────┐
│                         │
└─────────────────────────┘
```

4 ... ZACCHAEUS

Jesus is going to Zacchaeus' house.
What path will He take?

Start Here

The mouths of babes ROY MITCHELL

NOTHING WITHOUT JESUS

Read Luke 19:1-10. Now look carefully at the cartoon on the page opposite. The boy lists a lot of things he wanted. Do you think Zacchaeus had all these things before he met Jesus?

He may have had:

Lots Of Money ✔
Success ✔

But lots of money and success did *not* bring him:

Total Happiness ✗
Security ✗
Popularity ✗

Zacchaeus only found these *after* he had met Jesus and received Him as his Saviour! Without Christ and His salvation you will never know what true happiness, success or security really are. (Read Matthew 6:33).

THAT'S MY TREE!

Look up the Bible references to see *who* was linked with which tree. Enter the names in the grid - outlined letters will spell the name of another tree.

Juniper (1 Kings 19:4)
Palm (Judges 4:5)
Sycamore (Luke 19:4)
Fig (John 1:48)
Oak (2 Samuel 18:9)

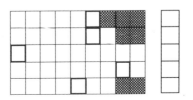

5 ... THE GOOD SAMARITAN

Can you find the Good Samaritan?
WHICH MAN of the three pictured
went to the rescue of the man
who was beaten by thieves and left for dead?

MATCH THE PAIR

Which TWO PICTURES are exactly the same?

a.

b.

c.

d.

THE CITY OF JERICHO

JERICHO was an important city in Old Testament times. The Israelites captured it under the leadership of Joshua - but it later fell under the judgment of God.

The name "Jericho" means "the place of fragrance." It never became that again until Jesus visited it. Here he transformed the lives of both Zacchaeus and Bartimaeus.

SOMETHING TO FIND

Can you find a map of Israel (perhaps in the back of your Bible) and locate where Jericho is?

KEY QUESTION NO.19

Name the TWO men who saw the injured man but did nothing to help him?

(You'll find the answer in Luke chapter 10)

ANSWER:

HELP-HIM-OUT!

Luke 10:30 tells us that the man who was helped by the 'Good Samaritan' had been on a journey to Jericho. Can you guide him through the maze to the city of Jericho?

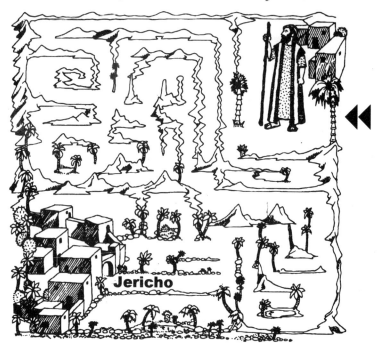

Jericho

KEY QUESTION NO.20

The man helped by the Good Samaritan was travelling to Jericho FROM WHICH CITY?

(a) BETHLEHEM
(b) NAZARETH
(c) JERUSALEM

ANSWER:

MUDDLED FACTS!

The man who was rescued by the Good Samaritan begins to tell his story to the inn-keeper. But his thoughts are still muddled. Read Luke 10:30-37 and correct the six mistakes in what he said.

"I was going from Jerusalem to Nazareth and was attacked by thieves. As I lay dying by the roadside, 2 merchants came along and talked to me. Then a travelling Egyptian showed kindness to me: he treated my wounds with oil and honey, set me on his animal and brought me to this inn. I hear he has paid 10 talents for my stay here already."

_____
_____
_____
_____
_____
_____
_____

RIGHT OR WRONG?

Other people listened to the man's story - and got mixed up about it too. Sort out what is right and wrong from the four sentences below.

YOU WILL FIND ALL YOUR ANSWERS IN THE STORY OF
THE GOOD SAMARITAN ...Luke 10:25-37.

- A lawyer asked Jesus who his neighbour was
- The priest did what he could to help
- Three pence was paid to the innkeeper for his care
- The Samaritan treated the wounds with oil and wine

Jesus said to Pilate: "Thou couldest have no power at all against me, except it were given thee from above" (John 19:11).

Why was our Lord Jesus Christ willing to die on the cross?

To find out the answer, cross out all D's, F's, G's, I's, J's, K's, N's, P's, Q's, R's, T's, W's, X's, Y's, and Z's.

D	B	I	E	Q	C	I	A	U	S	I	E
I	H	N	P	E	W	Q	Z	Y	J	G	X
G	L	D	F	O	V	I	J	E	K	S	N
M	D	Q	I	K	N	R	T	E	Y	P	I

_____

_____

The body of Jesus was laid in Joseph of Arimathea's tomb before His resurrection. Using the letters in the name

ARIMATHEA

how many words of 2 and more letters can you make?

❑ **Up to 35**   - **Good**
❑ **36-65**   - **Very Good**
❑ **66-98**   - **Excellent**
❑ **99+**   - **GENIUS!**

TRUE OR FALSE?

If the statement is **true**, circle the letter in the True column.
If the statement is **false**, circle the letter in the False column.

True	False	
⁶ **U**	¹ **S**	Jesus rose from the dead on the first day of the week.
¹ **S**	⁷ **E**	The soldiers were bribed by the priests to lie, and say that Jesus' disciples had stolen His body.
⁵ **O**	⁴ **N**	The angel's message was, "He is not here, but is risen."
³ **P**	² **A**	Early in the morning, Mary Magdalene and the other Mary went to Jesus' tomb, carrying flowers.
⁶ **T**	⁷ **R**	The angels rolled a large stone in front of the entrance to the tomb where Jesus lay.
⁴ **I**	⁵ **E**	The tomb that Jesus' body lay in for three days was borrowed.
² **W**	³ **V**	Peter and John were the first of Jesus' followers to see their risen Lord.

BONUS PUZZLE

Take the letters you have circled above and fit them into the squares below, matching the number of the square with the number beside the letter.

Remember how the angels announced the birth of Christ using this title? The fact that Jesus died and rose again fulfils this promise made by those angels at the time of Jesus' birth.

MAJOR DETECTIVE WORK!

Take a close look at JOHN 20:1-24 to find out what these people saw on the first Easter Day.

ⓘ	STONE ROLLED AWAY	INSIDE THE TOMB	THE ANGELS OF GOD	THE RISEN CHRIST
MARY				
PETER				
JOHN				
THOMAS				
OTHER DISCIPLES				

KEY QUESTION NO.21

Which disciple won the race to get to the tomb of Jesus on the first Easter morning? (Check ... John 20)

(a) JOHN
(b) PETER
(c) THOMAS

ANSWER:

All answers found in Acts 12:1-19

1. Prayer meeting for Peter was held in her house
2. Number of chains Peterl was bound with
3. Made of iron
4. Damsel at door
5. The king who killed James
6. "You"
7. His surname was Mark

DID YOU KNOW?

The Roman night was divided into four parts, called "watches." During each watch (or shift) four soldiers kept guard over Peter. Peter was chained to two of these; the other two acted as first and second guard at the doors of the prison.

(A quarternion=four soldiers)

KEY QUESTION NO.22

Acts 12:7 notes: "And his chains fell off from his hands."
Which gospel hymnwriter penned the words:
'My chains fell off, my heart was free;
I rose, went forth, and followed Thee'

❑ Emily E.S. Elliott (1836-1897)
❑ Isaac Watts (1674-1748)
❑ Charles Wesley (1707-1788)

MOUNTING THE RESCUE

How did the angel get to Peter in the prison?

OUR GOD IS ABLE TO DELIVER

Daniel in the Old Testament ... Peter in the New Testament - both of these men proved it! Proved what? That our God is able to deliver those who love Him, trust Him, live and suffer for Him.

Peter himself later wrote (after his tremendous deliverance from prison recorded in **Acts 12:1-19**): *"The Lord knoweth how to deliver the godly out of temptations"* (**2 Peter 2:9**). He certainly does!

Keep going on with God: He is able to deliver you from everything that threatens to harm you!

GENERAL
Testing your knowledge about many Bible subjects

1... WHO WROTE WHAT?

Can you match the Bible books
with the men who wrote them?

Genesis		Solomon
Lamentations		John
Revelation		Moses
Ecclesiastes		Paul
Galatians		Jeremiah

FIND THE BIBLE VERSE?

Build a verse
from the Psalms
by working
through
the clues
on the left.

Vague clue!
You will
find the answer
in either Psalm
48 or 84.

ASSEMBLING THE WORD

Name a drawing, add letters from one of the jumbled lines below - and you will find the complete word in the Bible verse.

1. CAPEC Isaiah 61:2
2. GNIPS John 4:14
3. LAYER 1 Corin. 12:31
4. SEE Hebrews 2:3
5. GRIN 1 Peter 5:8
6. SGR Matthew 7:16
7. NONIOCS Titus 3:9
8. DROAMA Ephesians 6:20

_____ _____ _____

_____ _____ _____

A STRAIGHT LINE TO JESUS

Ever heard of Moscow? Many years ago, when the railway was being made between the cities of Moscow and St. Petersburg, one of the old Emperors of Russia asked a large number of engineers to draw up the plans for it.

The Emperor checked the plans himself. They were quite complicated. Eventually he put them all to one side and said, "Bring me a ruler." A ruler was brought. He lifted a pencil, and, drawing a straight line between the two cities, he said, "This is the way to make it: we do not want any other plan than one straight line."

Many people are trying to get to heaven. They try many different paths. But the only path that leads there is this one - 'Draw a straight line to Jesus at once'! Jesus said (John 14:6), "I am the way ... no man cometh unto the Father but by Me."

Complete the wheel using the following clues

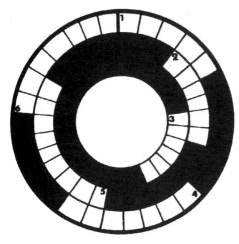

FILL IN THE SPACES ACCORDING TO THE CLUES. THE LAST TWO OR THREE LETTERS OF ANSWER NO.1 ARE THE SAME AS THE FIRST TWO OR THREE OF ANSWER NO.2, ETC.

1. Leader of the Exodus
2. Valley known for its large clusters of grapes (Numbers 13)
3. Mount from which Jesus ascended into heaven
4. Father of Queen Jezebel (1 Kings 16)
5. Coppersmith who did Paul much evil (Acts 19)
6. Paul sent him to Macedonia (Acts 19)

KEY QUESTION NO.23

Which Old Testament prophet saw a vision of wheels within wheels?

(a) ISAIAH
(b) EZEKIEL
(c) DANIEL

••• CLUE •••
You'll find the answer in
the FIRST CHAPTER of the prophet's book

ANSWER:

SPOT THE DIFFERENCE

Spot the 10 DIFFERENCES between the two pictures -
and then colour in the second pic

Which Israelite soldier led his army against the
Midianites armed with trumpets and earthern pitchers
with lamps inside them?

Joshua ☐   **Gideon** ☐   **David** ☐

WORDS IN THE WATERPOT

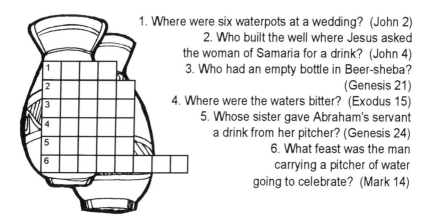

1. Where were six waterpots at a wedding? (John 2)
2. Who built the well where Jesus asked the woman of Samaria for a drink? (John 4)
3. Who had an empty bottle in Beer-sheba? (Genesis 21)
4. Where were the waters bitter? (Exodus 15)
5. Whose sister gave Abraham's servant a drink from her pitcher? (Genesis 24)
6. What feast was the man carrying a pitcher of water going to celebrate? (Mark 14)

DO YOU KNOW?

Why Jesus told His disciples to follow a man carrying a pitcher of water to find the Upper Room in Jerusalem?

FIND THE BIBLE VERSE

_____

_____

Guide the Shepherd to his Sheep

YOU & I ARE LIKE THAT LOST SHEEP
ISAIAH 53:6:

"All we like sheep have gone astray; we have turned every one to his own way; and the Lord hath laid on Him the iniquity of us all."

GOOD & BAD SHEPHERDS

□ I R E □ I N □

The Lord Jesus Christ is described as a Shepherd in the Bible.

He is:
The **GOOD** Shepherd,
The **GREAT** Shepherd,
and The **CHIEF** Shepherd.
John 10:11&14
Hebrews 13:20
1 Peter 5:4

Jesus described the man who left the sheep to the mercy of the wolf as ... ?

KEY QUESTION NO.24

Who is the FIRST shepherd named in the Bible?

(a) ADAM
(b) ABEL
(c) AARON

ANSWER:

Acts 27:12 tells us how Paul's ship tried to reach
the safety of Crete to spend the winter.
Guide that ship to its safe haven.

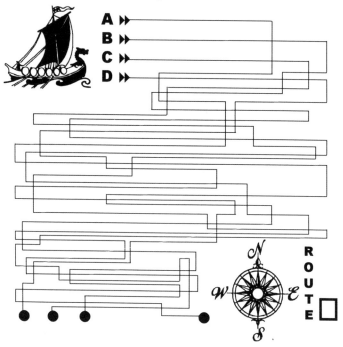

A ⯈
B ⯈
C ⯈
D ⯈

R
O
U
T
E

N
W E
S

GOOD NEWS!

*"... Though your sins be as
scarlet, they shall be as
white as snow; though they
be red like crimson, they
shall be as wool"* (Isaiah
1:18). Sin is cleansed
through the blood of Jesus.
This *is* GOOD NEWS!

STAYING FOR WINTER

Discover some cities Paul was connected with in winter. The letters in the shaded squares spell something we always associate with winter.

☐☐☐☐☐☐☐■☐	Titus 3:12
■☐☐☐☐☐☐	1 Corinthians 16:5&6
☐☐■☐☐☐☐	Acts 27:12

What we always associate with winter: _ _ _ .

WINTER RESIDENCE

Name the King who had a Winter house? (Jeremiah 36:22)

____

KEY QUESTION NO.25

Which man killed a lion in a pit on a snowy day? (1 Chronicles 11 will help you here!)

- ☐ **SAMSON**
- ☐ **DAVID**
- ☐ **BENAIAH**
- ☐ **DANIEL**

5 ... LIGHTS

A BURNING LAMP

Write your answers into the squares in the picture
to complete the lamp

CLUES

1. At what time did Aaron light the lamps? (Exod.30)
2. Who is the light of the world? (John 10)
3. Who came to bear witness of the Light? (John 1)
4. Complete: "Thy .... is a lamp unto my feet" (Psalm 119)
5. Where shall we need no light? (Revelation 22)
6. What kind of oil was used in the tabernacle lamp? (Exod. 27)

A SHINING LIGHT

Which friend of Jesus was described as "a burning and a shining light"?

(Check John 5:35)

We, too, are to be shining lights for Jesus in this dark world.

Shining for Jesus in a world of sin;
Shining for Jesus, bringing lost ones in;
Shining for Jesus, glorifying Him;
Shining all the time for Jesus.

ANSWERS

Solutions to all the Puzzles

N.B. Only use this to check your own answers - or when you're REALLY stuck!!!

GOD'S CREATION

p10: **Mountains**
1. Ararat 2. Carmel 3. Sinai
4. Moriah

Our God Has Made ...

```
    L  I  G  H  T
       O  R  I  O  N
       S  E  A
  P  L  E  I  A  D  E  S
  L  E  V  I  A  T  H  A  N
```

p11: Signpost:
Bethany, Bethphage, Jerusalem

Mount of Olives is a sabbath day's journey from Jerusalem (Acts 1:12).

Disciples: Peter, James & John
. . . .

p12: **Rivers of the Bible**
Arnon, Abana, Euphrates, Jordan, Kishon, Jabbok

4 rivers flowed out of Eden

Key Question 1: (b) Jordan.
. . . .

p13: **Plants of the Bible**

Shadow matching the flower - 3

8 Plants/ Trees in wordsearch are: Cedar, Olive, Lily, Rose, Fig, Sycamore, Mint and Corn.

Key Question 2: (c) Lilies.
. . . .

p14: **Trees of the Bible**

DOWN
1. Cypress

ACROSS
1. Cedar 2. Ebony 3. Poplar
4. Juniper 5. Elm 6. Aloes
7. Sycamore
. . . .

p14: **Birds of the Bible**
Owl, Dove, Eagle, Stork, Quail, Hen, Raven, Swallow, Heron, Sparrow, Ostrich, Pelican
. . . .

p15: **Dinosaurs**

DOWN
1 Cypress

ACROSS
1 Cedar 2 Myrtle 3 Pine
4 Juniper 5 Hazel 6 Chesnut
7 Sycamores

Key Question 3: (a) Behemoth

p17: Who Was Here First?
A,C & D have been around the longest! Each of these was created on DAY 5 (Genesis 1:20-23).

All land animals (including dinos) were created on DAY 6! (Genesis 1:24-31).

p17: Spot The Difference (Dino)

1 Eyes half closed 2 wrinkle below right eye 3 extra tooth on lower jaw 4 scales on back 5 spots 6 shorter arm 7 belly button 8 fatter tail 9 extra toe 10 missing claw on foot

. . . .

p20: **The Human Body**
1 Stomach 2 muscles 3 bones 4 arteries 5 joints 6 heart 7 kidneys 8 blood 9 elbows 10 intestines

Key Question 4: (b) Lev. 17:11

Key Question 5: (c) Psalm 139

. . . .

NOAH'S ARK ... FLOOD

p25: Noah's Ark Wordsearch

Part of Proverbs 3:5 spelt out by extra letters: "Trust in the Lord with all thine heart."

p26: Ark Wordsearch ... Facts & Figures about Noah's Ark

1. Gopher 2. Side 3. Three 4. Cubits 5. Height

p27: Homing Instinct

Answer: Flight Path 2

Key Question 6: (c) 3 (Genesis 8:8-12).

p28: Ark Crossword

ACROSS
1. Flood 5. Ark 6. Baa 8. Ru 10. Forty

DOWN
2. La 3. Orb 4. Okay 7. Fro 9. Ur

p29: Two By Two: Find The Pair

The matching pair is 2 and 5

Key Question 7: (b) 40

OLD TESTAMENT HISTORY

p33: **Joseph**

Across
4 Banquet 6 Benjamin 8 Famine
9 Food 10 Judah

Down
1 Egypt 2 Jacob 3 Cup
5 Simeon 7 Joseph

The Captain of Pharaoh's guard was Potiphar.

Key Question 8: (b) 20

. . . .

p35: **Moses**

Plotting the path to the Promised Land

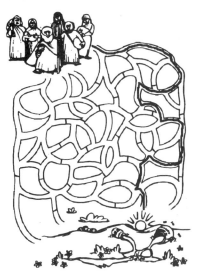

p35: Moses and the Psalms ... Psalm 90

p36: Match The Scrolls
b & f ... c & g ... d & e.

Key Question 9: (c) 187.

. . . .

p38: **Joshua**

10 Differences in Jericho picture

1 Man on left missing half his tongue 2 Man on left added circle on hat 3 Man in middle has mouth added 4 Man in middle has a striped shirt 5 Man on right with a shorter spear 6 Man on right missing ear 7 Different letter on flag 8 An extra spear among walls 9 One falling block missing 10 Added window to centre building

Key Question 10: 13 times

p39: Crossword: Words in Wall

Down
1 Scarlet 2 Zabdi 3 Achan 5 Ad
8 Seven 10 Once 11 Son

Across
2 Zerah 4 Rahab 6 Gold 7 Ai
8 Sihon 9 Token 11 Six 12 Cue
13 Gate 14 Nun

p40: A Message in Code

"I will not fail thee."

. . . .

p41: **Samson**

Which Town Is It? ... Ashkelon

Some Stats About Samson

1. 30 2. 3 3. 20 4. 1000 5. 7
6. 40 Total 1100

Key Question 10: (d) 1100

. . . .

p43: **Ruth**

Wordsearch - In The Grid

p43: Important Message From Boaz

"At mealtime come thou hither, and eat of the bread, and dip thy morsel in the vinegar."

p44: Spot The Difference

1 Man on left without headband
2 Lower man on left without cap
3 Mouse without tail 4 Strap missing from man's sandal (giving shoe)
5 Shadow on ground missing (in front of man giving shoe) 6 Armband missing from man giving shoe
7 Window behind archway missing
8 Dust missing under man receiving shoe 9 Missing brick in wall on right archway 10 Hair coloured black on man on bottom right of picture

p44: Which Harvest was it? ... The Barley Harvest

. . . .

p45: **David**

Crossword

1 David 2 Saul 3 Music 4 Goliath
5 Armour 6 Trusted 7 Shepherd

p45: Bonus Puzzle: Psalms

p47: Trace The Bible Verse

"The Lord saveth not with sword and spear: for the battle is the Lord's."

Key Question 12: (b) Loaves, corn and cheese

p48: Which Route For David?

A-E-G-B-D-H-F-C-A

p48: Map Reading

D ... Engedi
E ... Jerusalem
G ... Bethlehem
H ... Hebron

Key Question 13: Psalm 142 and Psalm 57.

p50: Rearrange The Letters

"The Lord Is My Shepherd."

Number of Psalms which begin with the Word "Blessed" ... 6

Key Question 14: (a) Boaz

p51: **Esther**

There are 13 Differences between the 2 Pictures.

127 Provinces in the kingdom of Ahasuerus.

p52: In Prison!

Bigthan & Teresh ... No, they were Hanged ... Mordecai saved his life.

Key Question 15: (a) Haman

p53: **Daniel**

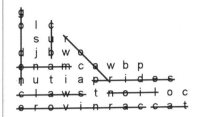

Key Question 16: The Angel of the Lord

p54: **Jonah**

How Many Days? ... 3

p54: A Book of 'Great' Things

Wind - tempest - fish - city - kindness ... Jonah was sleeping in the SIDES of the ship.

p55: Old Test. "J" Books ... 5

p56: A Vital Message in Code:

"Salvation is of the Lord" (Jonah 2:9).

p56: Jonah Wordsearch

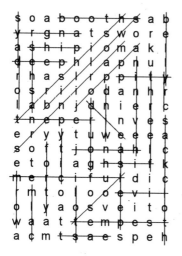

NEW TESTAMENT HISTORY

p59: **Jesus: His Birth**

Wordsearch

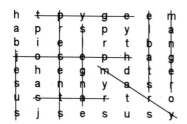

The Birth of Christ is recorded by 2 of the gospels.

Key Question 17: (b) Nazareth.

p60: Decode Secret Message:

"Call His name Jesus for He shall save His people from their sins" (Matthew 1:21).

. . . .

p61: **The Disciples of Jesus**

1 Disciples 2 Sandals 3 People
4 Twelve 5 Evil 6 Villages

p61: Missing Disciples

James ... Simon ... Judas (brother of James)

p62: Which Disciple? ... Peter

. . . .

p63: **Feeding of the 5000**

Wordsearch

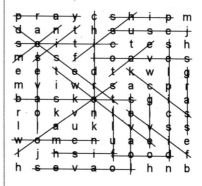

Key Question 18: (a) Two.

94

p64: **Zacchaeus**

p65: That's My Tree!

Elijah ... Deborah ... Zacchaeus ... Nathanael ... Absalom

Hazel

. . . .

p66: **The Good Samaritan**

Can You Find ... ?
He is the man on the right

p66: Match the Pair
... a & c.

Key Question 19: Priest & Levite.

p68: Help Him Out!

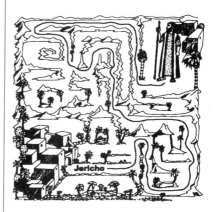

Key Question 20: (c) Jerusalem.

p69: Muddled Facts

Jericho ... a Levite and a priest ... passed by on the other side ... Samaritan ... wine ... two pence.

p69: Right or Wrong?

The first three are wrong; the last statement is correct.

. . . .

p70: **Death And Resurrection**

"Because He loves me."

p71: True Or False?

True - True - True - False - False - True - False

Bonus Puzzle: Saviour

p72: Major Detective Work!

Mary saw ... stone rolled away, inside the tomb, the angels of God and the risen Christ.

Peter and John saw ... inside the tomb and the risen Lord.

Thomas saw ... nothing.

The other disciples saw ... the risen Lord.

Key Question 21: (a) John.

p73: **Peter in Prison**

Crossword

1 Mary 2 Two 3 Gate 4 Rhoda
5 Herod 6 Ye 7 John

Key Question 22: Charles Wesley (1707-1788)

p74: Mounting The Rescue

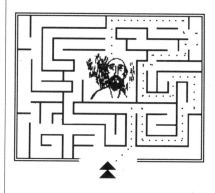

GENERAL

p77: **Who Wrote What?**

Genesis ... Moses
Lamentations ... Jeremiah
Revelation ... John
Ecclesiastes ... Solomon
Galatians ... Paul

p77: Find The Bible Verse

"For the Lord God is a sun and shield: the Lord will give grace and glory" (Psalm 84:11).

p78: Assembling The Word

1 Acceptable 2 Springing
3 Earnestly 4 Escape
5 Roaring 6 Grapes
7 Contentions 8 Ambassador

p79: **Wheels And Waterpots**

1 Moses 2 Eshcol 3 Olivet
4 Ethbaal 5 Demetrius 6 Erastus

Key Question 23: (b) Ezekiel.

p80: Spot The Difference

1 Pot on top left has a handle
2 Pot beside it changed design
3 Pot, centre left, moved
4 Bowl, bottom left, overlapping seat
5 Different pot in potter's hand
6 One pot less on shelf, top right
7 Bowl, centre right, now empty
8 Pot, bottom right, cracked
9 Pot beside it with lip design
10 Small pot beside potter's wheel

p80: Israelite Soldier ... Gideon.

p81: Words In The Waterpot

1 Cana 2 Jacob 3 Hagar
4 Marah 5 Laban 6 Passover

A man carrying a pitcher would stand out in the crowd because in those days this was looked on as a woman's job!

p81: Find The Bible Verse

"He that trusteth in the Lord, mercy shall compass him about" (Psalm 32:10).

p82: **Shepherds**

Guide the Shepherd ...

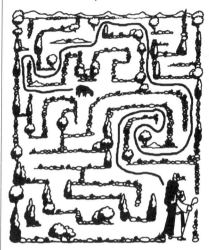

p83: Good And Bad Shepherds:
man who left the sheep to the mercy of the wolf is an Hireling (a hired servant who has no real interest in the sheep).

Key Question 24: (b) Abel.

. . . .

p84: **Winter**

Route B for Paul's ship

p85: Staying For Winter

1 Nicopolis 2 Corinth 3 Phenice

Associated with winter ... Ice.

p85: Winter Residence:

Jehoiakim

Key Question 25: Benaiah.

p86: **Lights**

A Burning Lamp

1 Even 2 Jesus 3 John
4 Word 5 Heaven 6 Olive

A Shining Light: John the Baptist

QUICK QUIZ
Key Questions 1-25

If you want to speed through the topics covered in this book by means of a Quick Quiz, then follow the path of the KEY QUESTIONS throughout the book. They are numbered 1-25. The first one is found on page 12. In most cases, the questions are in multiple choice format. See how you score ... .

1.	p12	☐	14.	p50	☐
2.	p13	☐	15.	p52	☐
3.	p16	☐	16.	p53	☐
4.	p20	☐	17.	p59	☐
5.	p21	☐	18.	p63	☐
6.	p27	☐	19.	p67	☐
7.	p29	☐	20.	p68	☐
8.	p34	☐	21.	p72	☐
9.	p37	☐	22.	p73	☐
10.	p38	☐	23.	p79	☐
11.	p42	☐	24.	p83	☐
12.	p47	☐	25.	p85	☐
13.	p49	☐	Total		